Pebble® Plus
Bilingüe/Bilingual

Máquinas maravillosas/Mighty Machines
Trenes/Trains

por/by Matt Doeden

Traducción/Translation: Dr. Martín Luis Guzmán Ferrer

Editor Consultor/Consulting Editor: Dra. Gail Saunders-Smith

Consultor/Consultant: Bob R. Tucker
General Manager of Train Handling (Retired)
Railway Operating Officers Association

Capstone

Mankato, Minnesota

Pebble Plus is published by Capstone Press,
151 Good Counsel Drive, P.O. Box 669, Mankato, Minnesota 56002.
www.capstonepress.com

1 2 3 4 5 6 13 12 11 10 09 08

Library of Congress Cataloging-in-Publication Data
Doeden, Matt.
    Trenes = Trains / by Matt Doeden.
    p. cm. — (Máquinas maravillosas = Mighty machines)
    Includes index.
    ISBN-13: 978-1-4296-2374-2 (hardcover)
    ISBN-10: 1-4296-2374-8 (hardcover)
    1. Railroads — Trains — Juvenile literature. 2. Locomotives — Juvenile literature. I. Title. II. Title: Trains.
III. Series.
TF148.D64 2009
625.1 — dc22   2008001256

Summary: Simple text and photographs describe trains, their parts, and what they do — in both English
    and Spanish.

Editorial Credits
Mari Schuh, editor; Katy Kudela, bilingual editor; Eida del Risco, Spanish copy editor; Molly Nei, set designer;
    Patrick D. Dentinger, book designer; Jo Miller, photo researcher/photo editor

Photo Credits
Corbis/Morton Beebe, cover; Premium Stock, 17; Richard T. Nowitz, 14–15
David R. Frazier Photolibrary Inc., 4–5
The Image Finders, 8–9, Howard Ande, 10–11, 19
Lynn M. Stone, 6–7
PhotoEdit Inc./Jeff Greenberg, 12–13
Shutterstock/Ryan Parent, 1; Wade H. Massie, 20–21

Note to Parents and Teachers

The Máquinas maravillosas/Mighty Machines set supports national social studies standards
related to science, technology, and society. This book describes and illustrates trains in
both English and Spanish. The images support early readers in understanding the text.
The repetition of words and phrases helps early readers learn new words. This book also
introduces early readers to subject-specific vocabulary words, which are defined in the
Glossary section. Early readers may need assistance to read some words and to use the
Table of Contents, Glossary, Internet Sites, and Index sections of the book.

Table of Contents

Tabla de contenidos

Trains

A train is a long line
of railroad cars
hooked together.
Trains move on tracks.

Trenes

El tren es una fila larga
de vagones de ferrocarril
enganchados entre sí.
Los trenes se mueven
sobre rieles.

Parts of Trains

Trains have wheels that fit over railroad tracks. Railroad tracks are long steel rails.

Las partes de los trenes

Los trenes tienen unas ruedas que se ajustan a los rieles. Los rieles del ferrocarril son unas largas barras de acero.

Locomotives pull trains.
The train's engine sits
inside the locomotive.

Las locomotoras tiran de
los trenes. El motor del tren
está dentro de la locomotora.

Railroad cars make up
the longest part of a train.
Freight cars carry goods.
Passenger cars carry people.

Los vagones de ferrocarril
forman la parte más larga
del tren. Los vagones de carga
llevan mercancías. Los vagones
de pasajeros llevan personas.

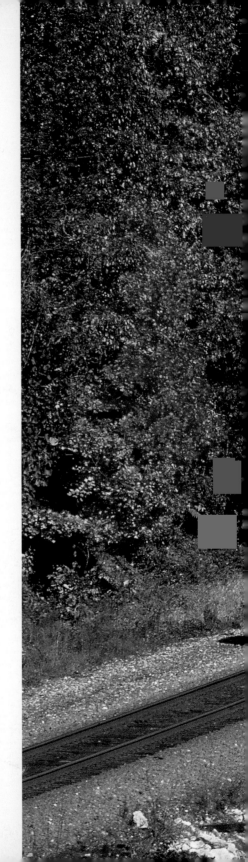

10

Choo! Choo!

Trains have loud whistles.

Whistles warn people

that a train is coming.

¡Chu! ¡Chu!

Los trenes tienen unos silbatos

muy ruidosos. Los silbatos

les avisan a las personas

que el tren se acerca.

Kinds of Trains

Commuter trains carry

people on short trips.

Subway trains run

under city streets.

Tipos de trenes

Los trenes suburbanos llevan a

las personas en viajes cortos.

Los trenes del metro corren

bajo las calles de la ciudad.

14

15

Passenger trains carry people

for thousands of miles.

People can eat and sleep

on these trains.

Los trenes de pasajeros llevan

a las personas a miles de millas

de distancia. Las personas pueden

comer y dormir en esos trenes.

Freight trains carry coal,
grain, and other goods
across the country.

Los trenes de carga llevan
carbón, granos y otras
mercancías a través del país.

Mighty Machines

Trains roll through tunnels
and under bridges. Trains
are mighty machines.

Máquinas maravillosas

Los trenes pasan por los túneles
y bajo los puentes. Los trenes
son máquinas maravillosas.

Glossary

freight train — a train that carries goods or cargo; some freight trains are more than a mile long.

goods — items that people buy and use; freight trains carry goods such as car parts, toys, and food.

locomotive — the railroad car that holds the engine to pull the train

subway train — a kind of train that runs under the ground

track — a set of rails for trains to run on

tunnel — a passage made under the ground or through a mountain for use by trains and cars

whistle — an object that makes a high, loud sound; cars and trucks should not cross railroad tracks when a train is blowing its whistle.

Glosario

la locomotora — el vagón de ferrocarril que tiene el motor que tira del tren

las mercancías — artículos que la gente compra y usa; los trenes de carga llevan mercancías como piezas de autos, juguetes y alimentos.

el metro — tipo de tren que corre bajo tierra

el riel — juego de vías sobre las que corre el tren

el silbato — objeto que hace un sonido fuerte y alto; los autos y los camiones no deben cruzar las vías del tren cuando el tren hace sonar el silbato.

el tren de carga — tren que lleva mercancías o carga; algunos trenes tienen más de una milla de largo.

el túnel — pasaje bajo tierra o que cruza una montaña, construido para que puedan pasar trenes y autos

Internet Sites

FactHound offers a safe, fun way to find Internet sites related to this book. All of the sites on FactHound have been researched by our staff.

Here's how:

1. Visit *www.facthound.com*

2. Choose your grade level.

3. Type in this book ID **1429623748** for age-appropriate sites. You may also browse subjects by clicking on letters, or by clicking on pictures and words.

4. Click on the **Fetch It** button.

FactHound will fetch the best sites for you!

Index

Sitios de Internet

FactHound te brinda una manera divertida y segura de encontrar sitios de Internet relacionados con este libro. Hemos investigado todos los sitios de FactHound. Es posible que algunos sitios no estén en español.

Se hace así:

1. Visita *www.facthound.com*

2. Elige tu grado escolar.

3. Introduce este código especial **1429623748** para ver sitios apropiados a tu edad, o usa una palabra relacionada con este libro para hacer una búsqueda general.

4. Haz un clic en el botón **Fetch It**.

¡FactHound buscará los mejores sitios para ti!

Índice